SIMPLE GUIDES

VERY SIMPLE SPANISH

ABOUT THE AUTHOR

VICTORIA MIRANDA McGUINESS was born in Madrid
and spent her formative years in León in northern Spain.
Later, she lived in Chicago before settling in England. She is
a regular visitor to Spain and is currently Senior Lecturer in
Spanish at New College, Durham.

VERY SIMPLE

SPANISH

VICTORIA McGUINESS

GLOBAL BOOKS LTD

Simple Guides • Series 2
VERY SIMPLE LANGUAGE

VERY SIMPLE SPANISH
By Victoria McGuiness

First published 1995 by
GLOBAL BOOKS LTD
PO Box 219, Folkestone, Kent, England CT20 3LZ

ISBN 1–86034–002–4

British Library Cataloguing in Publication Data
A CIP catalogue entry for this book
is available from the British Library

Distributed in the USA & Canada by:
The Talman Co. Inc
131 Spring Street
New York N.Y. 10012
USA

Set in Futura 11 on 12 point by Bookman, Slough
Printed in Great Britain by
The Cromwell Press Ltd, Broughton Gifford, Wiltshire

Contents

Foreword

where Spanish is spoken

Spanish is spoken by some 400 million people in more than twenty different countries. It is the official language in Spain and in all of Central and South America with the exception of Brazil. It is widely spoken in Ecuatorial Guinea, Morocco, Western Sahara, the Philippines and increasingly, by more than 20 million people, in the United States of America. It is also used by many Jewish people of Sephardic origin in parts of Turkey, Greece and Israel.

Spanish is a world language and it has many different accents which give it its richness and variety. What I have written for you is the standard version of Spanish, also known as 'castellano', because it originated in Castilla, the central region of Spain. When you know how to express yourself in Castilian, therefore, you will be understood everywhere Spanish is spoken.

If you already know Portuguese, French, Italian or Romanian, you will find Spanish easy to learn. Like those languages, Spanish derives from Latin, so its grammatical structure is not too different from theirs. The vocabulary is also quite similar to these languages. Another point of interest is the fact that five per cent of Spanish words come from Arabic – a reminder of the 800 years the Arabs were in Spain and of their contribution to the Spanish language and civilization.

Spanish is also quite easy to learn for complete beginners. It was the first Romance language to have a written set of grammatical rules as compiled by Antonio de Nebrija in his *Gramática de la Lengua Castellana* published in 1492. But those rules can be realistically simplified without distortion of meaning, so that beginners do not need to feel daunted in the early stages. And because Spanish is a phonetic language it is one of the most approachable to start on your own.

Do your studying when you are feeling relaxed, you will assimilate things faster. Also, you will memorize new words better if you learn a few each day instead of attempting long study periods.

I hope you will find this little book as useful and user-friendly as my students do.

¡Que te diviertas! (Have fun!)

V.M.M.
DURHAM
November 1994

A Quick Guide to Pronunciation

Spanish is very easy to learn because it is a phonetic language: each letter represents a sound which is always pronounced in the same way.

Pronounce vowels as follows:

a as in apple   = _Ana, fiesta_
e as in elephant = _elefante_
i as in Lisa   = _vino, mi_
o as in on   = _Rosa, patio_
u as in put   = _tu, mucho_

Pronounce most consonants as you would in English with the following exceptions:

c followed by e/i sounds like the _th_ in 'thin' in Castilian Spanish, otherwise like the c in 'cent', 'cinema'

h is always silent

ch sounds like the ch in 'chair'

j sounds like the English h in 'ham'

g followed by e/i also sounds like the English h in 'ham'

ll sounds like the English y in 'yes'

ñ sounds like the ni in 'onion'

q is always followed by u, but this u is silent as in 'mosquito'

r is rolled softly

rr is rolled strongly

v sounds like an English *b* in Castilian Spanish, otherwise like the English *v*

z sounds like the *th* in 'thin' in Castilian Spanish, otherwise like the English *z*

VOWEL COMBINATIONS OR DIPHTHONGS

ie   sounds like the English *ye* in 'yes'
EXAMPLES: f*ie*sta, s*ie*sta

ue   sounds like the English *we* in 'wet'
EXAMPLES: f*ue*go (fire), b*ue*no (good)

STRESS

Words ending in a *vowel* or the consonants *n* or *s* are stressed on the penultimate syllable.

EXAMPLES: *vi*no, *Ro*sa, *Car*men

Words ending in a *consonant*, (except *n* or *s*) are stressed on the last syllable.

EXAMPLES: ho*tel*, nacionali*dad*, a*mor*

Any exceptions to these rules are indicated by a written accent.

EXAMPLES: avi*ón*, in*glés*

Written accents are also used to differentiate between words with the same spelling but different meaning.

EXAMPLES: *tú* (you) *tu* (your)
            sí (yes) *si* (if)
            Yo *hablo* (I speak) El *habló* (he spoke)

Written accents are also used when the stress falls on the antepenultimate syllable.

EXAMPLES: mag*ní*fico, es*tú*pido

Basic Grammar

1. NOUNS

All nouns are either feminine or masculine. Most FEMININE nouns end in -**a**, -**ad**, -**ión**.

EXAMPLES: *Fiesta* (party), *nacionalidad*, (nationality), *habitación* (room)

Most MASCULINE nouns end in -**o**, or in a consonant.

EXAMPLES: *vino* (wine), *hotel* (hotel)

But there are exceptions.

EXAMPLES:
mano (hand), ends in -**o** but is feminine
día (day), ends in -**a** but is masculine
avión (plane), ends in -**ión** but is masculine

2. PLURALS

Words ending in a vowel (a,e,i,o,u) add -**s**.

EXAMPLE: *fiesta* (party), becomes *fiestas* (parties)

Words ending in a consonant (any letter which is not a vowel) add -**es**

EXAMPLE: *hotel* (hotel), becomes *hoteles* (hotels)

3. ARTICLES

'A' = *un* (masculine) EXAMPLE: *un hotel* (a hotel).

= *una* (feminine) EXAMPLE: *una fiesta* (a party).

'**The**' *el* (masculine, singular) EXAMPLE: *el hotel* (the hotel)

los (masculine, plural) EXAMPLE: *los hoteles* (the hotels)

la (feminine, singular) EXAMPLE: *la fiesta* (the party)

las (feminine, plural) EXAMPLE: *las fiestas* (the parties)

4. ADJECTIVES

These describing words always go after the noun and agree with it, which means that if the noun is feminine and singular, the adjective will have to be feminine and singular.

EXAMPLES: *vin**o** buen**o*** (good wine)
*vin**os** buen**os*** (good wines)
*fiest**a** buen**a*** (good party)
*fiest**as** buen**as*** (good parties)

If the adjective ends in -e or in most consonants, there is no change in gender

EXAMPLES: *fiesta interesant**e*** (interesting party)
*vino interesant**e*** (interesting wine)
*fiesta fenomena**l*** (wonderful party)
*vino fenomena**l*** (wonderful wine)

But they still change in the plural.

EXAMPLES: *fiest**as** interesant**es*** (interesting parties)
*vin**os** fenomenal**es*** (wonderful wines)

5. POSSESSION

To indicate that something belongs to somebody you need the word *de*.

EXAMPLES: *La habitacion **de** Manuel* (Manuel's room)

*El vino **de** Rosa* (Rosa's wine)

6. POSSESSIVE ADJECTIVES

Two things to take into account:
– They agree with the thing possessed.

EXAMPLES: **mi** fiesta (my party), but **mis** fiestas (my parties)

– There are two forms for 'your': **tu** is informal, **su** is formal.

EXAMPLES: **tu** vino (your wine when talking to a friend)
su vino (your wine, when talking to a stranger)

Singular possessives: **mi** (my) **tu** (your, informal) **su** (his, her, your, formal)

Plural possessives: **mis tus sus**

EXAMPLES: **mi** habitación (my room)
mis habitaciones (my rooms)
tu hotel (your hotel)
tus hoteles (your hotels)
su vino (his wine, her wine, your wine, formal)
sus vinos (his wines, her wines, your wines, formal)

7. PRONOUNS

These come in several varieties and are usually placed before the verb.

a) PERSONAL PRONOUNS: They indicate who is doing something (i.e. the subject in the sentence). They are as follows:

yo	I
tú	you (informal)
él	he (or it for a masculine object)
ella	she (or it for a feminine object)
usted	you (formal)

EXAMPLES: Yo hablo español (I speak Spanish)
Ella habla español (she speaks Spanish)

b) OBJECT PRONOUNS: They indicate who or what is the recipient of the action (i.e. the object in the sentence).

They are as follows:

c) DIRECT OBJECT PRONOUNS:

me	me
te	you
lo	him, it
la	her, it

EXAMPLES: *Juan me quiere* (Juan loves me)
Yo te quiero (I love you)
Yo la quiero (I love her)
Yo lo veo (I see him/I see it – masculine object)
Yo la veo (I see her/I see it – feminine object)

d) INDIRECT OBJECT PRONOUNS:

me	to me
te	to you
le	to him, to her

EXAMPLES: *Rosa me escribe* (Rosa writes to me)
Rosa te escribe (Rosa writes to you)
Rosa le escribe (Rosa writes to him/her)

8. VERBS

Spanish has a rich choice of grammatical moods and tenses, but I will only give you the three basic tenses which you will need for the present, the past and the future.

Since we spend most of our conversations talking about ourselves (I=*yo*), addressing our friends (you=*tu*, informal; *usted*, formal) or gossiping about them (he=*él*, she=*ella*), I am going to give you only these bits of the verb to make learning easier. If, however, you feel that you want to address a crowd or use the royal 'we', you can always refer to a conventional grammar book and look under: *nosotros* (we, us), *vosotros* (you, all), *ellos* (they, them).

Verbs change the endings to indicate by whom and when an action or activity is being performed. When you look up a verb in the dictionary you will find it in its infinitive form.

EXAMPLE: Comer (to eat)
If you want to say 'I eat' you have to drop the final two letters -er and add -o and you get: Yo como (I eat).

REGULAR VERBS

These come in two groups:
Verbs ending in -ar like hablar (to speak, to talk)
Verbs ending in -er like comer (to eat) or in -ir like vivir (to live)

HOW TO TALK ABOUT THE PRESENT (What you do, what you are doing)

Hablar = To speak

yo	hablo	(I speak)
tú	hablas	(you speak, informal)
él	habla	(he speaks)
ella	habla	(she speaks)
usted	habla	(you speak, formal)

From now on, I will not give you the end for usted (which becomes Vd. in abbreviation) since it always has the same ending as el/ella.

Comer = To eat

yo	como	(I eat)
tú	comes	(you eat)
él/ella	come	(he/she eats)

EXAMPLES: comprar (to buy), trabajar (to work) will follow the pattern for hablar.

vivir (to live), escribir (to write), beber (to drink), will follow the pattern for comer.

HOW TO TALK ABOUT THE PAST (What you did, what you have done). *See Chapter 12.*

HOW TO TALK ABOUT THE FUTURE (What you are going to do). *See Chapter 13.*

IRREGULAR VERBS

These do not follow the patterns above, so they have to be learnt individually. The most commonly used are *ser* (to be), *estar* (to be somewhere), *ir* (to go), *tener* (to have), *hacer* (to do, to make), *querer* (to love, to want). You still have to remove the *-ar/-er/-ir* endings and add the corresponding ones. I will give you them as the verbs pop up in context in later chapters.

9. NEGATIVES

No, means both no and not, and goes before the verb

EXAMPLE: *yo no bebo* (I do not drink).

10. WORDS FOR ASKING QUESTIONS

¿*Qué?* =   What?
¿*Quién?* =   Who?
¿*Cuál?* =   Which one?
¿*Cómo?* =   How?
¿*Cuándo?* = When?
¿*Dónde?* =   Where?
¿*Por qué?* = Why?

All questions and exclamations are written with two question/exclamation marks.

EXAMPLES: ¿*Qué?* =   What?
         ¡*Hola!* =   Hello!

3

Su Nombre, Por Favor:

Personal Identification/ Meeting People/ Filling Forms

Verbs for this unit:

Hablar (regular)= to speak.

Llamarse (reflexive)= to be called. This is a regular verb. Like all reflexives, it ends in -se. Remove the last two letters and add the corresponding endings as follows:

   yo me llamo (I am called, my name is)

   tú te llamas (you are called, your name is)

   él/ella se llama (he/she is called, his/her name is)

Ser (irregular) = to be.
yo *soy*　　(I am)
tú *eres*　　(you are)
él/ella *es*　(he/she is)

GREETINGS AND FAREWELLS

¡Hola!　　= Hello!, Hi! Reply = *¡Hola!*
Buenas　　= Good morning/afternoon/evening.
　　　　　　Reply= *Buenas.*
¿Qué tal? = How are things?
Just as in English for this one you always reply:
Bien, ¿y tú? = Fine, and how are you?
Hasta luego/Hasta la vista = See you later
Adiós　　　= Goodbye

INTRODUCTIONS

When meeting someone for the first time, shake hands and say:

Mucho gusto = pleased to meet you

To introduce your friends say:

Este es mi amigo Fernando/Este es Fernando
=This is my friend Fernando/This is Fernando
Esta es mi amiga Paloma/Esta es Paloma =This is my friend Paloma/This is Paloma

TALKING ABOUT YOURSELF

Me llamo Victoria　　　= My name is Victoria
Soy inglesa　　　　　　= I am English
Hablo español　　　　　= I speak Spanish
Hablo español bien　　 = I speak Spanish well
No hablo español　　　 = I do not speak Spanish
Me defiendo en español = I get by in Spanish

The adjective for the foreign language is the same as the adjective for the male inhabitant of the corresponding country.

A MAN would say:

Soy inglés y hablo inglés = I am English and I speak English

Soy italiano y hablo italiano = I am Italian and I speak Italian

A WOMAN would say:

Soy inglesa y hablo inglés = I am English and I speak English

Soy italiana y hablo italiano = I am Italian and I speak Italian

Notice that adjectives are never written in capital letters:

Soy de Manchester = I am from Manchester

Mi amiga es profesora = My friend is a teacher

Yo no soy marinero = I am not a sailor (a line from 'La Bamba' song)

ASKING OTHERS ABOUT THEMSELVES

¿Cómo te llamas? = What is your name?

¿Eres americano? = Are you American? (when asking a man)

¿Eres americana? = Are you American? (when asking a woman)

¿Hablas español? = Do you speak Spanish?

¿Tu amigo es inglés? = Is your friend English?

The statement is the same as the question: 'eres de Londres' means 'you are from London'; '¿eres de Londres?' means 'are you from London?' This is the reason for having the extra question mark at the beginning. In speech raise your voice at the end when asking questions.

FILLING FORMS

You will find the following words when asked to fill in a form or to supply information about yourself in a formal situation:

Nombre = Name

Apellidos = Surname
Nacionalidad = Nationality
Dirección/Domicilio = Address
Fecha de nacimiento = Date of birth
Lugar de nacimiento = Place of birth
Profesión = Occupation
Firma = Signature
Número de pasaporte = Passport number
Marca del coche = Make of car
Matrícula del coche = Car registration number
Carnet de conducir = Driving licence
Alojamiento = Accommodation

When asked for a document say:
'*Aquí tiene*' (Here you are) as you hand it in.

*   *   *

...and a few more words

No sé = I don't know
No entiendo = I don't understand
Más despacio = Say it again, more slowly
Por favor = Please
Gracias = Thank you
De nada = Don't mention it/You are welcome
Vale = O.K.

4

¿Qué hora es?:
Time & Numbers/ Seasons & Weather

Hace sol

Verbs for this unit:

Trabajar (regular) = to speak

Tener (irregular) = to have
yo *tengo*   (I have)
tú *tienes*   (you have)
él/ella *tiene*   (he/she has)

NUMBERS

First learn numbers 0 to 20

0	cero	**3**	tres
1	uno	**4**	cuatro
2	dos	**5**	cinco

(Find the rest of the numbers in the reference section)

Then learn the tens from 20 to 90

20   veinte   **40**   cuarenta
30   treinta   **50**   cincuenta

(Find the rest in Chapter 14)

Now combine tens and units to suit your needs:

34   treinta y cuatro
45   cuarenta y cinco
51   cincuenta y uno
and so on.

100 cien is one hundred. After that it works as follows:

200 doscientos (if the objects you are counting are masculine, as in 'dólares', you say 'doscientos dólares'; if the objects are feminine as in 'pesetas', you say 'doscientas pesetas')

300 trescientos/trescientas
800 ochocientos/ochocientas
and so on.
The odd one out is
500 quinientos/quinientas.

1.000   mil. It is the easiest one to work out.
2.000   dos mil
3.000   tres mil
10.000   diez mil
40.000   cuarenta mil
and so on.

TELLING THE TIME

To find out the time ask:

¿Qué hora es? = What time is it?
And you will hear first the hour and then the minutes.

EXAMPLES:
  Las dos y diez = It's ten past two OR
  Las dos menos diez = It's ten to two

This is a diagram of how it works:

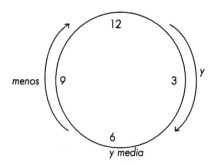

To find out when things are happening ask:
  ¿A qué hora? = At what time?/When?

EXAMPLES:
  ¿A qué hora trabajas? = At what time/When do you work?
  A las dos y media = At half past two
  Yo trabajo a las ocho menos cuarto = I work at quarter to eight

MEASURING TIME

Por la mañana/por la tarde = In the morning/in the afternoon
Ayer, hoy, mañana = Yesterday, today, tomorrow
Un día, un año = A day, a year
El lunes/los lunes = On Monday/on Mondays
En enero/en julio = In January/in July

EXAMPLES:
  No trabajo los domingos = I don't work on Sundays
  Trabajo mucho el lunes = I work a lot on Monday

Notice that days of the week and months of the year are not written with capital letters.

Years are treated as ordinary numbers.

EXAMPLE:
   1992 is = *mil novecientos noventa y dos*

SEASONS AND WEATHER

Find out what the weather is like in your favourite holiday resort by asking:

¿Qué tal hace (en Málaga)? = What is the weather like (in Malaga)?

And you might hear:

En verano hace calor = It's hot in summer
En invierno llueve = It rains in winter

Except for 'it rains' (*llueve*) you will hear '*hace*' with the weather.

EXAMPLES:
   Hace frío = The weather is cold
   Hace sol = It's sunny
   Hace bueno = The weather is fine/It's a fine day
   Hace malo = It's not a nice day
   Hace calor = It's hot

BUT if it is you who is cold or hot, you need to say it with '*tener*'.

EXAMPLES:
   Tengo frío = I am cold
   ¿Tienes calor? = Are you warm?

*　　*　　*

...and a few more words

Mucho = Much, a lot
Poco = A little
Y = And
Pero = But
También = Also

*   *   *

Turn to Chapter 14 for a complete list of days, months and seasons of the year.

5

¿Cuánto es?
Weights & Measures/ Shopping/Banks & Services

Verbs in this unit:

Comprar (regular) = to speak

Querer (irregular) = to want
yo quiero = I want
tú quieres = you want
él/ella quiere = he/she wants

WEIGHTS & MEASURES

Things are measured in:

kilos (about 2 lbs)
litros (about 2 pints)
kilómetros (about 3/4 of a mile)

BUYING FOOD

If you prefer not to have to speak to anybody when you go shopping, go to the supermarket (*el supermercado*). In smaller, specialized shops ask for what you need like this:

Dos kilos de patatas = two kilos of potatoes
Medio kilo de tomates = half a kilo of tomatoes

You can also ask for individual items like this:

Dos pasteles = two cakes
Un melón   = a melon

Or you can mention the containers in which they come:

EXAMPLES:
Una botella de vino   = a bottle of wine
Un paquete de mantequilla = a packet of butter
Una lata de sardinas   = a tin of sardines
Una caja de bombones   = a box of chocolates

When you finish your transaction ask:

¿Cuánto es? = How much is it?

BUYING CLOTHES AND SHOES

Size is *'talla'* for clothes
         'número' for shoes
Talla 38 is size 8 in clothes
Talla 40 is size 10 and so on.
Número 35 is size 4 in shoes
Número 36 is size 4½ and so on.

EXAMPLES:
You are size 14 and want to buy three teeshirts so you ask for:

'Tres camisetas, talla 44'
You want a pair of shoes and you take size 10, so you ask for:
'Un par de zapatos, número 47'.

To get exactly what you want in clothes you need to know about colours. Remember they are adjectives, therefore, they will have to agree with the noun they qualify.

EXAMPLES:
camiseta roja = red teeshirt
zapatos rojos = red shoes

(Find more colours in Chapter 14)

BANKS AND SERVICES

The easiest way to pay for goods and services in Spain is by VISA credit card/debit card, either of which you can use to draw pesetas from VISA cash points. If you want to change your own currency or travellers cheques go to a bank where, in many cases, you will have to ring the bell to gain access. Once inside look for the counter with the word 'CAMBIO' (exchange) on it and say:

Quiero cambiar cheques de viaje = I want to change travellers cheques
Quiero cambiar libras/dólares = I want to change £s/$s

To buy stamps for your cards or letters you can go to the post office ('Correos') or a tobacconist ('un estanco') which has a red T advertising itself. Ask for:

dos sellos   *para Inglaterra* *para postal* =
(two stamps) (for England) (for a card)
un sello   *para Italia* *para carta* =
(a stamp) (for Italy) (for a letter),
and so on.

Mail boxes ('un buzón') are painted yellow.

*   *   *

...and a few more words

Así	= Like this
Más	= More
Menos	= Less
Más o menos	= More or less
Basta	= That's enough
Grande	= Big, large
Pequeño	= Small
Para mí	= For me
Para tí	= For you
Para él	= For him
Para ella	= For her
Abierto	= Open
Cerrado	= Closed

6

¿Dónde esta?
Getting Around/Public & Private Transport

¿Dónde?

Verbs for this unit:

Ir (irregular) = to go
yo voy   = I go
tú vas   = you go
él/ella va = he/she goes

Estar (irregular) = to be somewhere
yo estoy   = I am (somewhere)
tú estás   = you are (somewhere)
él/ella está = he/she is (somewhere)

UNDERSTANDING DIRECTIONS

Whent you ask

'¿Dónde está el banco?'
el hospital?'
el restaurante?'

you might get a long and complicated set of directions. In that case say the phrase you already know so well: 'Más despacio, por favor' and you will find that most directions will be simplified to:

aquí = here
allí = there
todo recto = straight on
a la derecha = on/to the right
a la izquierda = on/to the left

hasta (el semáforo   up to (the traffic lights
(el cruce   (the junction

Then find out how far it is:

'¿Está (lejos?   Is it (far?
(cerca?   (near?

And the response will come either in time or distance:

A dos kms./ A dos horas. = Two kms. away/ two hours away

GETTING AROUND

Most hotels will have street maps of their city. Ask:

¿Tiene un plano de Madrid? = Do you have a street map of Madrid?

For more information go to:

La oficina de turismo = The tourist office

Or look for information desks or offices at airports and public places under the ⓘ international sign.

USING PUBLIC TRANSPORT

AIRPORTS

You will not encounter any problem here. All signs at international airports directing you to passport control, customs and baggage reclaim are in Spanish and English. At smaller airports look for:

'Control de pasaportes' = Passport control, *'Aduana'* = Customs and *'Recogida de Equipaje'* = Baggage reclaim

TAXIS

Travelling by taxi is not expensive. Hail them down in the street or ask for them at your hotel:

Quiero un taxi, por favor = I would like a taxi, please

For long journeys, check the fare with the taxi driver before you set out by asking:

¿Cuánto es al aeropuerto? = How much is it to the airport?
¿Cuánto es al centro? = How much is it to the centre?

If you have a specific address in mind simply say:

Hotel Miramar, por favor = To the Miramar Hotel, please

TRAINS AND BUSES

To ask for the bus stop say:

¿Dónde está la parada del autobús?

And for the underground say:
¿Dónde está la boca del metro?

For inter-city travelling find out first where the stations are:

¿Dónde está la estación del tren? = Where is the railway station?

¿Dónde está la estación de autobuses? = Where is the bus station?

Once there ask for a timetable:

Un horario, por favor
and work out your journey at your leisure.

Travel times use the 24 hour clock. When ready to buy your ticket look for the ticket office under the words '*TAQUILLAS*' or '*BILLETES*' and ask for:

Un billete para Madrid de ida y vuelta ,
no fumador = A ticket to Madrid return, non smoker

Or:

Dos billetes para Sevilla de ida , fumador = Two tickets to Sevilla single, smoker

'*En primera*', '*En segunda*', mean first or second class. If you do not specify it will be understood that you want to travel second class.

TRAVELLING BY CAR

If you are thinking of hiring a car do it in your own country with the 'fly-drive' schemes which work out more cheaply. If you want to hire a car in Spain say:

Quiero alquilar un coche = I want to hire a car

And be prepared to fill in a form or answer questions like the ones you encountered in Chapter 3. Buy a road map (*Un mapa de carreteras*) and acquaint yourself with the different types of road.

*   *   *

... and a few more words

Salida   = Exit
Entrada   = Entrance
Salidas   = Departures
Llegadas = Arrivals
La primera = The first (road, exit, street, etc)
La gasolina = Petrol
La gasolinera = The petrol station
Lleno, por favor = Fill it up, please
Super/normal = High/low octane petrol
Sin plumo = Unleaded
Aceite multigrado = Multigrade oil
Autovía   = Dual carriageway
Autopista de peaje = Toll motorway

7

Quiero una habitación :
Booking Rooms & Holiday Accommodation

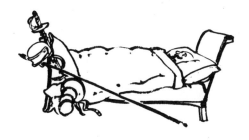

If you want information on camping sites or hotels write to the Spanish Tourist Office in your own country or to the Oficina de Turismo of the town you want to visit in Spain.

HOTELS

When you arrive in your hotel, having booked a room in advance, say:

Tengo una reserva a nombre de . . . (your name)
= I have a reservation. My name is . . .

If you have not booked in advance say:

Quiero una habitación doble/individual = I want a double/single room
para dos/tres (etc) noches = For two/three (etc) nights
con/sin baño (o ducha) = With/without a bath (or shower)

Then be ready to supply personal information about yourself either by filling in a form (*una ficha*) or by being asked the kind of questions you encountered in Chapter 3.

The price of the room will not include breakfast. Find out if there is a restaurant in the hotel ('*¿Hay un restaurante en el hotel?*'); or better still, find out if there is a cafe nearby ('*¿Hay una cafetería cerca?*') which will be cheaper and will provide better coffee than the hotel.

If you have a car, find out about parking:

¿Hay un aparcamiento en el hotel? = Is there a car park in the hotel?
¿Hay un aparcamiento cerca? = Is there a car park nearby?

At the end of your stay ask for the bill ('*La cuenta, por favor*'). If you want to pay with a credit card ask:

¿Se puede pagar con tarjeta? = Can I pay with a credit/bankers card?

CAMPING SITES

To book at a camping site say:

Quiero una plaza para una tienda = I want a place for a tent
          y un coche = and a car

and then say for how many nights and fill in similar forms to the one you have encountered when booking in a hotel.

* * *

...and a few more words

El hotel = the hotel
El camping = the camping site
IVA, impuestos, servicios = VAT, taxes, service charges
Hay . . . ? = Is there . . . ?/ Are there?
Con/sin = With/without
La llave = the key
El ascensor = the lift
El equipaje/ las maletas = the luggage/ the cases
El precio = the price
Los servicios = the toilets

8

Me gusta Madrid :
Likes & Dislikes/
Entertainment & Holidays

Me gusta Madrid

Verbs for this unit:

Vivir = to live (regular)

Hacer = to do, to make (irregular)
yo hago = I do (I make)
tú haces = you do (you make)
él/ella hace = he/she does (he/she makes)

Gustar = to like (regular and always used with indirect pronouns)
me gusta = I like (literally: 'it pleases me')
te gusta = you like (literally: 'it pleases you')
le gusta = he/she likes (literally: 'it pleases him/her')

EXAMPLES:

Me gusta el teatro/ el cine/ el deporte
I like the theatre/ the cinema/ sport

Le gusta el vino/ la coca-cola/ la paella
He/she likes wine/ coke/ paella

¿Te gusta Madrid? = Do you like Madrid?
Sí, me gusta mucho = Yes, I like it very much

Me gusta Carmen = I like Carmen.
No me gusta Juan = I don't like Juan

¿Qué te gusta hacer? = What do you like doing?
Me gusta bailar = I like dancing
Le gusta vivir aquí = He/she likes living here

Notice that when you like things you say *el/ la* in front of them. When you like people, you do not. When you like doing things you use the infinitive of the verb.

ENTERTAINMENT & HOLIDAYS

To be on holiday = *estar de vacaciones*

You already know the verb *ESTAR* from Chapter 6, so you could talk about things you like doing when you are on holiday.

EXAMPLES:
Cuando estoy de vacaciones, me gusta ir the excursion = When I am on holiday, I like going on trips

Vivo en Chicago pero estoy de vacaciones aquí = I live in Chicago but I spend my holidays here

Buy your tickets for your favourite show from the box office (*la taquilla*) by saying:

Dos entradas para el cine = two tickets for the
cinema

Dos entradas para el partido = two tickets for the match

Dos entradas para la discoteca = two tickets for the disco

* * *

...and a few more words

Me gusta mucho = I like it very much
No me gusta nada = I don't like it at all
Me encanta = I love it
Lo odio = I hate it
Es gratis = It's free
Es aburrido = It's boring
Es divertido = It's fun
¡Que te diviertas! = Have fun!/Have a good time!

9

La carta, por favor :
Bars & Restaurants/
Food & Drink

Verbs for this unit:

Beber = to drink (regular)
Comer = to eat (regular)

BARS & RESTAURANTS

You will never be stuck for something to eat or drink in Spain. Bars, restaurants and cafes are open all day and close quite late at night. Spanish people use them for meeting their friends for a 'second breakfast' around 11.00 am, or for a chat and a snack (*tapas*) before lunch or supper or indeed for a drink at any time of day, or a family meal on Sundays.

The best regional cuisine is to be sampled in the town's old district known as 'el casco antiguo' or 'el barrio antiguo'. If you are on a tight budget you can ask for the set menu 'el menú del dia' at a restaurant and have an inexpensive, satisfying meal, which will include bread and wine.

FOOD & DRINK

El desayuno (breakfast) is usually eaten between 9.00 and 11.00 am. Ask for:

Un café solo	= A black coffee
Un café con leche	= A milky coffee
Un té	= A cup of tea
Un té con limón	= Tea with lemon
Una tostada	= A hot toast with butter

If you want a more substantial breakfast ask for:

Huevos fritos con bacon = Fried eggs and bacon

La comida (lunch) is served between 2.00 and 3.00 pm. La cena (supper), between 9.00 and 10.00 pm. Ask for:

La carta = The menu

Many restaurants have the menu printed in several languages. If not, the main categories are:

Entremeses	= Hors d'oeuvre
Sopas	= Soups
Pasta	= Pasta
Verduras	= Vegetables
Pescado	= Fish
Carne	= Meat
Postre	= Dessert

To know how a dish has been cooked look for:

Frito = Fried

Asado = Roasted
A la plancha/ a la parrilla = Grilled

If you want to know what ingredients have been used ask:

¿Qué lleva ésto? = What's in this dish?

At the end of your meal ask for:

La cuenta = the bill
And leave 5–10% as a tip.

If you want a lighter meal have '*tapas*', the small snacks eaten in Spain with a drink before a main meal. They sometimes come free with your drink but if you want a bigger portion ask for:

Una ración de (*calamares* = A portion of (squid
(*gambas* = (prawns
(*cheese* = (cheese

And do not forget the drink:

Una cerveza = A beer
Una tónica = Tonic water

*   *   *

... *and a few more words*

Frío /Caliente = Cold / Hot
Salado = Salty
Soso = Bland, tasteless
Picante = Spicy
Con hielo = with ice
La propina = the tip
Agua mineral con/sin gas = Fizzy/still mineral water
Un fino = A dry sherry
Oiga, por favor = Excuse me, please
(to attract the waiter's or anybody's attention)

10

¡Dígame! :
Business Matters/ Phoning & Writing

Verbs for this unit:

Vender = to sell
Comprar = to buy
Exportar = to export
Importar = to import

all regular verbs

BUSINESS MATTERS

Businesses and shops usually open from 9.00 am until 1.30 pm and from 4.00 until 8.00 pm with a long lunch break in between. Some factories work round the clock in shifts ('*turnos*'). Most public offices use the continuous working day ('*jornada intensiva*') from 8.00 am until 3.30 pm. Banks close at 2.00 pm.

Many shops and offices close for part or the whole of August when you might see *'Cerrado por vacaciones'* ('Closed for the holidays') on the door. Spanish workers are entitled to 30 days paid annual leave.

Business deals might start with a working lunch (*'almuerzo de trabajo'*). Do not worry about your lack of fluency in Spanish if you are trying to buy; you might have to try harder if you are trying to sell. Translation and interpreting services are good, but do try to make the right impression by introducing yourself in Spanish. You already know how to do it since the basics were covered in Chapter 3. Here are a few suggestions, and remember to shake hands at the beginning and at the end of a meeting.

EXAMPLES:
Buenas, me llamo Sara Knowles = Hello, my name is Sara Knowles
Trabajo en 'Plastics and Polymers' = I work in 'Plastics and Polymers'
Soy directora / gerente / secretaria = I am a director / managing director / a secretary
La sede central está en Londres = The head office is in London
con sucursales en Madrid y Paris = with branches in Madrid and Paris
Mi compañía exporta a América = My company exports to America

And so on. You have enough verbs and information to be able to adapt the previous opening lines to suit your requirements. Do not forget to make the necessary changes for your occupation if you are a man, so that *'directora'* will become *'director'*, etc.

The worlds of technology, commerce and the media use words very close to their English equivalents: 'teléfono', 'computador' (although 'ordenador' is more common) or English terminology: fax, video, marketing, etc.

PHONING

Obviously, you will never be expected to answer the phone at this stage, but you might want to phone someone. The conversation will probably go like this:

EXAMPLE:
Receptionist: *¡Dígame!* = Hello, can I help you?
You: *Quiero hablar con el señor López* = I want to talk to Mr Lopez
Receptionist: *¿De parte de quién?* = Who is calling?
You: *Soy John Smith, de Londres* = I am John Smith, from London
Receptionist: *Un momento, por favor* = Just a moment, please

And let us hope that when Mr López comes to the phone he can speak English!

WRITING

Informal letters start:

Querido Rafael: / *Querida Isabel:* = Dear Rafael / Dear Isabel

and finish with:
Abrazos = Hugs (equivalent to 'love' in English letters)
Saludos = Greetings/ Regards

Use one or the other according to how effusive you are feeling.

Formal letters are blocked and start:

Estimado Sr. Lopez: = Dear Mr Lopez
Estimado Sr.: = Dear Sir
Estimada Sra. Lopez: = Dear Mrs Lopez
Estimada Sra.: = Dear Madam

and finish with:
Atentamente, = Yours sincerely/ Yours faithfully

* * *

...and a few more words

¿Cómo se dice en español? = How do you say it in Spanish?
Tengo (un problema = I have (a problem
    (una cita   =   (an appointment
    (una reunión =   (a meeting
Lo siento, el señor Lopez no está = I'm sorry, Mr Lopez is not in
Aquí tiene mi tarjeta de visita = Here is my card
Siéntese = Have a seat

11

No funciona :
When Things Go Wrong/ Police/ Medical Help

When things go wrong

Verbs for this unit:

Doler = to hurt
me duele = It hurts me
te duele = It hurts you
le duele = It hurts him/ her

Notice that this verb behaves like GUSTAR in Chapter 8.

Perder = to lose
yo pierdo = I lose
tú pierdes = You lose
él/ella pierde = he/she loses

Both verbs are regular, i.e. they have the same endings as verbs ending in -er but as you can see there is a slight change in the stem.

WHEN THINGS GO WRONG

'*No funciona*' is the notice you will see on machines or equipment which is out of order, so when things break out or stop working for you, mention them in Spanish followed by these two words.

EXAMPLES:
El coche no funciona = The car does not work
El water no funciona = the toilet does not work
La calefacción no funciona = the central heating does not work

POLICE

Watch out for pickpockets at airports and stations; particularly in the big towns. They are well organized and very professional, so hold on tight to your bag or wallet and keep your money separate from your credit cards/ travellers cheques, then if one goes missing, you still have the other for emergencies.

If you are robbed, go to the police station (*la comisaria*) and explain what has happened:

EXAMPLES:
Me han robado el pasaporte = My passport has been stolen
Me han robado el dinero = My money has been stolen

Or if you lose something:

Perdí la tarjeta de crédito = I lost my credit card
Perdí los cheques de viaje = I lost my travellers cheques

You will have to sign a formal statement to claim from your insurance company, so be prepared to answer questions similar to the ones in Chapter 3 about personal identification plus details of the incident.

EXAMPLES:
¿Dónde perdió el dinero? = Where did you lose your money?
En el aeropuerto, en el hotel = At the airport, the hotel
¿Cuándo perdió el dinero? = When did you lose your money?
Ayer, hoy = Yesterday, today

If things are or get complicated and you cannot find an English speaker at the police station, ask to ring your consular representative.

EXAMPLE:
Quiero telefonear al cónsul inglés/ americano/ canadiense/ etc.

If you commit a traffic offence, you will be fined and will have to pay on the spot (*'una multa'*).

MEDICAL HELP

Do take medical insurance back home. If you are an EC national get form E111 in your own country for free treatment in Spain. For minor ailments go to the chemist's, explain what is wrong with you and they will give you something for it.

EXAMPLES:
¿Tiene algo para el dolor de (*cabeza?*
(*muelas?*

Have you got anything for   (a headache?
(a toothache?

I f you need the doctor say: *Quiero un médico* (I want a doctor) and you could say:

Me duele el estomago = I have a stomach upset
Tengo fiebre   = I have a temperature.

Or if you are a hypochondriac you can always say:

Me duele todo = Everything hurts.

* * *

...and a few more words

¿*Qué pasa?* = What's the matter?/ What's wrong?
¿*Qué le pasa?* = What's wrong with you?
¿*Dónde le duele?* = Where does it hurt?
¿*Cuánto hace que le duele?* = How long has it been hurting you?

¿Qué hiciste ayer?
Chatting About the Past

The past

The following are the verb endings which you will need to talk about things you did or events that took place in the past.

REGULAR VERBS

Hablar (and all verbs ending in -*ar*)

yo hablé	= I spoke
tú hablaste	= you spoke
él/ella habló	= he/she spoke

EXAMPLES:
Hablé con mi hermana = I spoke to my sister
Trabajé mucho ayer = I worked a lot yesterday

Comer (and all verbs ending in -er and -ir)

yo comí	= I ate
tú comiste	= you ate
él/ella comío	= he/she ate

EXAMPLES:
¿Qué comiste? = What did you eat?
Fernando perdió el pasaporte = Fernando lost his passport

IRREGULAR VERBS

Ser and **Ir** share the same endings

yo fui	= I was/ I went
tú fuiste	= you were/ you went
él/ella fue	= he/she were/ he/she went

EXAMPLES:
La fiesta fue muy divertida = The party was great fun
Ella fue a Londres = She went to London

Estar

yo estuve	= I was	) somewhere
tú estuviste	= you were	)
él/ella estuvo	= he/she was	)

EXAMPLE:
¿Dónde estuviste ayer? = Where were you yesterday?

Decir

yo dije	= I said
tú dijiste	= you said
él/ella dijo	= he/she said

¿Qué dijo el medico? = What did the doctor say?

Tener

yo tuve	= I had
tú tuviste	= you had
él/ella tuvo	= he/she had

EXAMPLE:
No tuve problemas = I didn't have any problems

Hacer (Remember this verb can mean 'to do' or 'to make')

yo hice	= I did, I made
tú hiciste	= you did, you made
él/ella hizo	= he/she did, he/she made

EXAMPLE:

Ayer no hice nada	= I didn't do anything yesterday
¿Hiciste tu cama?	= Did you make your bed?

Querer

yo quise	= I wanted
tú quisiste	= you wanted
él/ella quiso	= he/she wanted

EXAMPLE:

Ella no quiso nada = She didn't want anything

¿Qué vas a hacer mañana?:

Planning for the Future

The future

The easiest way to talk about the future is to use the present tense of the verb **IR** ('to go'), which you learned in Chapter 6, plus an infinitive, which is very similar to what you do in English.

EXAMPLES:

Voy a comprar muchas cosas = I am going to buy many things

¿Dónde vas a pasar las vacaciones? = Where are you going to spend your holidays?

Marisa va a comer = Marisa is going to eat

Pepe va a trabajar en el jardín = Pepe is going to work in the garden

General Reference

COUNTRIES/ LANGUAGES/ PEOPLE

Australia, australiano = Australia, Australian
Canadá, canadiense = Canada, Canadian
España, español = Spain, Spanish
Estados Unidos, americano = USA, American
Inglaterra, inglés = England, English
Irlanda, irlandés = Ireland, Irish
Italia, italiano = Italy, Italian

NUMBERS

1	*uno*	11	*once*
2	*dos*	12	*doce*
3	*tres*	13	*trece*
4	*cuatro*	14	*catorce*
5	*cinco*	15	*quince*
6	*seis*	16	*dieciseis*
7	*siete*	17	*diecisiete*
8	*ocho*	18	*dieciocho*
9	*nueve*	19	*diecinueve*
10	*diez*	20	*veinte*

30	*treinta*	100	*cien*
40	*cuarenta*	1000	*mil*
50	*cincuenta*		
60	*sesenta*	*Primero*	= First
70	*setenta*	*Segundo*	= Second
80	*ochenta*	*Tercero*	= Third
90	*noventa*	*Cuarto*	= Fourth

COLOURS

blanco	=	white
negro	=	black
*gris**	=	grey
*marron**	=	brown
rojo	=	red
*naranja**	=	orange
amarillo	=	yellow
*verde**	=	green
*azul**	=	blue
*violeta**	=	violet

(Colours marked with the asterisk do not change gender.)

DAYS/ MONTHS/ SEASONS

lunes	= Monday		*enero*	=	January
martes	= Tuesday		*febrero*	=	February
miércoles	= Wednesday		*marzo*	=	March
jueves	= Thursday		*abril*	=	April
viernes	= Friday		*mayo*	=	May
sábado	= Saturday		*junio*	=	June
domingo	= Sunday		*julio*	=	July
			agosto	=	August
primavera	= spring		*septiembre*	=	September
verano	= summer		*octubre*	=	October
otoño	= autumn		*noviembre*	=	November
invierno	= winter		*diciembre*	=	December

Vocabulary

The following abbreviations apply:

adj = adjective
adv = adverb
conj = conjunction
interj = interjection
nf = noun, feminine
nm = noun, masculine
prep = preposition
pron = pronoun
v = verb

a (prep) – to
aeropuerto (nm) – airport
agua (nf) – water
abrazo (nm) – hug
aburrido (adj) – boring
aceite (nm) – oil
abierto (adj) – open
adiós (interj) – goodbye
ahora (adv) – now
alojamiento (nm) – accommodation
allí (adv) – there
alquilar (v) – to hire, to rent
americano (adv/adj) – American
año (nm) – year
apellido (nm) – surname
aquí (adv) – here
asado (adj) – roasted
ascensor (nm) – lift
así (adv) – like this
autopista (nf) – motorway
autovía (nf) – dual carriageway, freeway
ayer (adv) – yesterday

banco (nm) – bank
baño (nm) – bath, bathroom
basta (adv) – enough
beber (v) – to drink
bien (adv) – well
billete (nm) – ticket
botella (nf) – bottle
bueno (adj) – good
buzón (nm) – mail box

cabeza (nf) – head
café (nm) – coffee, coffee shop
calamar (nm) – squid
calefacción (nf) – central heating
calor (nm) – heat
cambiar (v) – to change
cambio (nm) – change, exchange
camiseta (nf) – teeshirt
carne (nf) – meat
carnet (nm) – licence
carta (nf) – letter, menu
cerca (adv) – near
cerrado (adj) – closed
cerveza (nf) – beer
cita (nf) – appointment
coche (nm) – car
comer (v) – to eat
comisaría (nf) – police station
compañía (nf) – company
comprar (v) – to buy
con (prep) – with
cosa (nf) – thing
cruce (nm) – junction
cuando (adv) – when
cuenta (nf) – bill

de (prep) – of, from
decir (v) – to say
desayuno (nm) – breakfast
día (nm) – day
dinero (nm) – money

dirección (nf) – address
director (nm) – director
divertido (adj) – fun, enjoyable
doble (adj) – double
dólar (nm) – dollar
doler (v) – to hurt
dolor (nm) – pain, hurt
domicilio (nm) – address
donde (adv) – where
ducha (nf) – shower

él (pron) – he
ella (pron) – she
empresa (nf) – firm
entender (v) – to understand
entrada (nf) – entrance
equipaje (nm) – luggage
eso (pron) – that
español (adv/adj) – Spanish
estación (nf) – station, season
estar (v) – to be (place or mood)
esto (pron) – this
estómago (nm) – stomach

fecha (nf) – date
firma (nf) – signature
frío (nm & adj) – cold
frito (adj) – fried

gamba (nf) – prawn
gasolina (nf) – petrol
gasolinera (nf) – petrol station
gerente (nm) – manager
grande (adj) – big
gustar (v) – to like

habitación (nf) – room
hablar (v) – to speak, to talk
hacer (v) – to make, to do
hielo (nm) – ice
hola (interj) – hello
hora (nf) – hour

horario (nm) – timetable
hospital (nm) – hospital
hotel (nm) – hotel
hoy (adv) – today
huevo (nm) – egg

individual (adj) – single
inglés (adv/adj) – English
italiano (adv/adj) – Italian
ir (v) – to go

kilo (nm) – kilogramme
kilómetro (nm) – kilometre

lejos (adv) – far
leche (nf) – milk
libra (nf) – pound sterling
limón (nm) – lemon
litro (nm) – litre
luego (adv) – later
lugar (nm) – place
llamarse (v) – to be called
llegada (nf) – arrival

mal (adv) – badly
malo (adj) – bad
mañana (nf) – morning
mañana (adv) – tomorrow
mantequilla (nf) – butter
marca (nf) – brand name, make
más (adv) – more
medio (adj) – half
melón (nm) – melon
menos (adv) – less
mi (adj) – my
matrícula (nf) – registration number
multa (nf) – fine
mucho (adv/adj) – much, a lot

nacionalidad (nf) – nationality
no (adv) – no
noche (nf) – night
nombre (nm) – name

número (nm) – number

oficina (nf) – office

para (prep) – for
parada (nf) – bus stop
pasaporte (nm) – passport
pastel (nm) – cake
patata (nf) – potato
pequeño (adj) – small
pero (conj) – but
perder (v) – to lose
pescado (nm) – fish
picante (adj) – spicy
plano (nm) – street map
poco (adv) – little
postal (nf) – postcard
postre (nm) – dessert
precio (nm) – price
profesión (nf) – occupation
propina (nf) – tip

que (conj/pron) – what, which
querer (v) – to want, to love
queso (nm) – cheese
quien (pron) – who

reserva (nf) – reservation, booking
restaurante (nm) – restaurant
reunión (nf) – meeting
robar (v) – to steal

salado (adj) – salty
salida (nf) – exit, departure
saludo (nm) – greeting
sardina (nf) – sardine
sello (nm) – stamp
semana (nf) – week
señor (nm) – man, gentleman
señora (nf) – woman, lady
ser (v) – to be
servicio (nm) – service, toilet
sí (adv) – yes

sin (prep) – without
sol (nm) – sun
sopa (nf) – soup
soso (adj) – bland
su (adj) – his/hers

talla (nf) – size
también (adv) – also
tapa (nf) – snack
tarjeta (nf) – card
té (nm) – tea
tener (v) – to have
tienda (nf) – tent, shop
tomate (nm) – tomato
tostada (nf) – toast
trabajar (v) – to work
tú (pron) – you (familiar)
tu (adj) – your

usted (pron) – you (formal)

vender (v) – to buy
vino (nm) – wine
vivir (v) – to live

y (conj) – and
yo (pron) – I

zapato (nm) – shoe

NOTES/VOCABULARY